Cloak Of Dawn

SILENT VOICE

NGOZI P. UMAJIE

Library of Congress Control Number: 2011907796
ISBN: Hardcover   978-1-4628-6850-6
                Softcover   978-1-4628-6849-0
                Ebook   978-1-4628-6851-3

This book was printed in the United States of America.

To order additional copies of this book, contact:
Xlibris Corporation
1-888-795-4274
www.Xlibris.com
Orders@Xlibris.com
96615

Cloak Of Dawn

Contents

The Quest for a Greener Life

The thought and the reality of travelling to America as a young lady was a dream come true, especially since I came from a village that could be hardly identified in the map at that particular era.

This is my story as a young girl who, in all my young life, thought and dreamt about the journey to the bigger world different from my small world called Oshiugbokor in the eastern part of Nigeria. It was also known then as the Niger Delta. Life in the sixties for me was nothing much to remember except for a few, such as my mother getting me and my other siblings ready for a journey to her motherland to escape from the soldiers. But Daddy walked into his room, came out, and announced that the journey was cancelled. This actually was a disappointment for me as a child because I wanted to see the other part of the world.

In the seventies, my adventure in the outside world progressed as I journeyed to the only known city in my community called Ahoada in Ekpeye Land. I was delighted with the sounds of generators and cars. Electricity was exciting, and the engaging atmosphere was all I had always dreamed of and envisioned. It was the adventurous world. Oh, what a dream come true! Furthermore, in the late seventies, I finally settled in the city called Ahoada with my eldest sister, Grace, who as a result of marriage, was taken out of the family at a very young age. Only God and my parents knew the age and the conditions to make a young girl to be suitable for marriage. But to me, it was dandy. I could, as a result, travel to a bigger and brighter world than the one I was born into. Although I loved my village and all that was in it, there was this quest for a bigger and brighter world.

In the eighties, I proceeded farther as my parents' interest of sending the children to higher learning other than elementary school, increased. I eventually settled in a city called Port Harcourt, the oil city or commonly referred to as the garden city. It was a city where life has no end. Although power outage was frequent, it was still 100 percent better than the city I left behind in terms of civilization and socialization. One would wonder about the excitement. Who would want to wake up every morning sweeping a compound, making breakfast, or journey four or more miles back and forth for farming engagement? Then you would come home late in the evening with a basket load of firewood on your head, which was a lifestyle and means of livelihood. You would do this except on the market days in other villages and Sundays, when you rest after returning from church.

My world seemed complete when one summer day while travelling back to the city from my village, I met this handsome man who swept me off my feet and promised me all that I had ever dreamt of. That was the beginning and the end of my quest for migration to a better life in America.

The promise of that day was one I would never forget. I waited and anticipated even more for almost ten years for my faithful and prospective savior to make my dream come true by marrying me and bringing me to the United States of America. For me, it was a country where everybody is portrayed as living the good life. Even the animals the people hunt on daily basis appeared to be treated better than humans. I thought 'How exciting for me was the American dream.'

However, the American journey turned out to be nothing but life unimaginable. You could never comprehend world until you have lived your life in the United States of America. My dream and quest turned out to be a nightmare, so I have decided to share my story with the world. This, of course, would be buttressed in some of my poems as you read.

In the early nineties, my dream came true as I migrated to the United States. I could hardly tell anyone about my departure to the United States of America because of the fear that somebody somewhere might prevent me from travelling. Nobody knew except my immediate family, my Papa and Mama, Mary, and my best friend Charity, commonly known as Chacha. Others found out later, probably few days after I had departed the country. But it was a shattered dream as I would discover later. The man who promised me love, later turned to be my tormentor. Tears became my companion. Life became lies; joy turned into anguish and dark dreams. There were unstoppable nightmares, unresolved marriage issues, and fights. I was constantly slapped around. The stories were unimaginable, and I received threats of being killed, yet no one knew. I had no relatives to run to or cry to and no means of returning back. I was trapped in the world I so much dreamt about. The dream was shattered the very first night I arrived into the United States. First, there was no food ready after that long journey. There were no welcome hugs and kisses like I had anticipated. I waited for him for so long at the airport. He showed but the greeting was cold as he only said hi to me and when I inquired why, I was given a laundry list of excuses, and I earnestly bought those excuses. But the best was yet to come.

The journey I anticipated to be brief and enjoyable pending a quick visit back home, became a life sentence in a foreign land without any family member. The man who professed to be the man for me turned out to be my worst nightmare, and I began to ask why. He had no answers but mockery and laughter. I constantly asked, "Am I paying for my sins of disobeying God? Could God be that mean?" I sometimes would ask, but inside I knew that was not God but the angel of darkness. My life was never and had never been the same from the very day I arrived in this great country.

The bitter truth was that a month after my arrival, I was pregnant. This was supposed to be a blessing for any couple, especially if love was practiced and expressed. However, mine was rather a boot camp, a slave-and-master relationship. "What has gone into him?" I would say and report to his family members, but all I heard was "That is him." "Oh, I thought I can't and I won't live this way, not me!" The unofficial marriage lasted for just six years, which was like twenty years of torture and torment. Nevertheless, it resulted in the birth of two awesome and wonderful boys. Yes, for a country I so much dreamt about and longed for, I would have done anything including marriage, but now it's something I detest. What an awful moment and experience! I wondered what and where to go but there was none.

The situation was so tensed that I began to ask for help. I remembered a particular instance when I was threatened by one of his cousin's by the name A. who was also living with us at that time. "If he is locked up, you and your son have to find another place to live." I then contacted the only family I knew in the United States of America. First she agreed and arranged on how I could get to her in the morning by train with then my only child. How excited I was. But few hours into the night of our planned departure, Mrs. E., whom I commonly referred to as Ms. J., called me back with a clause stipulated by her husband. His condition was that, he would allow me to move in with her family if my so-called husband gave me a letter stating that he no longer wanted me as a wife. I asked why and she stated that her husband would not like to be accused of taking someone's wife. It was a moment of despair, confusion, pain, overwhelming sorrow, and unstoppable tears. My dream of survival was minimized, and hope became far-fetched. Loneliness was eminent. What a price to pay for my sins. I felt lost, lonely and abandoned in a foreign country. My so-called sweetheart turned out to have a bitter heart. Had I known, I would have never seized the moment.

I remembered an instance when the Montgomery County Police got involved and even pressed charges on my behalf, but the case would not move forward because I would not testify against him for the abuse. I begged on his behalf, especially after knowing that I and my son would have nowhere to go and nobody to provide for us. But the abused unrecognized husband by the legal law of the land, since he had from the beginning advised me not to with reasons best known to him.

This went on, and the fear of being deported was eating me up that I would not still own up while being interrogated during a counseling session that was ordered by the Montgomery County Department of Social Services through a court order by the judge in one of our family court appearances. The experience drained me so much. If it wasn't for the Christian upbringing and my faith in Christ in the midst of the turmoil, I would have personally gone insane.

In another episode, I reached out to a village man known back home but now resided in the States. I would simply refer him as Mr. U. E. He also turned me down. His reason was that I already have a son with my husband. What an arrow. What have I done to deserve such a treatment from a man, who with reasons best known to him, came to Nigeria across the ocean, with all his effort, and paved my way to the world's greatest country? In my case it was love at first sight—or so I thought. Even after few years later when I found love outside my-then fiancée, I could not recognize it for the love of America or the thought of travelling outside the country. The sense of adventure was overshadowed with what I later knew as love that in the late eighties. It then resulted to travelling to meet my so-called American husband. What a twist of fate as queen ship is taken away in a brief moment as you travel millions of miles away from home in the quest for a better life.

My life was like one of the movies, although I had never watched, dreamt, or envisioned such. The worst was my husband's family. No one seemed to intervene, and the only one who really acted as an in-law was attacked constantly by his own brother, my so-called husband. None of them seemed to care, not even the brother who was a lawyer. I will always remember what he said to me when I complained to him about his brother's treatment," My brother said a woman has to be treated this way, So, let me see how he would treat his own and it will work for him."

This story needed to be told so that the world would not rush to jumping into the plane for a better future while what they left behind might be better. This is also to prevent such agony that most foreigners suffer from the mouths and hands of people who promise to offer them better life, the torture some foreigners go through in such lands of promises and dreams.

My strengths were God and my first son. I kept on remembering his first smile after his birth. It was magical, although at his birth his father was not present but one of the sisters. "He's filled with thick grown hair," the nurses and doctor said as he came. They cleaned him up before bringing him to me. With pain, agony, anger, and disappointment, I slowly looked up to see him. For the first time, I saw the smile on his face. I was perplexed and flabbergasted and was shocked in disbelief to see the smile on the young baby's face. It was an awesome moment that changed my life forever. For my first son, I decided to have another child just to give him a sibling to play with. At that moment though, I had made up my mind that I will not live the rest of my life in that torturous environment or condition for my son's sake. He deserved a brother or sister even after the shot I was given by the department of health to prevent me from conceiving another child. They didn't tell me many details. A lady just walked into my room and told me to sign a paper to prevent such pregnancy in the future since my child was born out of wedlock, but it was a miracle. I conceived my second son. Until now I still believe that the injection they gave had not taken effect in my system since I conceived my second son. However, I almost lost my baby because by the time I went for my last trimester visit, my baby was not showing any movement. Dr. Magid asked me to call my husband right away so that he could take me to the emergency room at Holy Cross. My blood pressure was way high up, and my son was not doing well either. It resulted to an immediate delivery. I would not forget that fateful day as once again I was left alone in the theater room with a bunch of nurses and doctors without my husband. His excuse was he had to watch our first son. What happened to the rest of his family who could easily watch the child? At that moment, I knew the chapter is closed and that the future is unknown. I had to thank the Oprah Winfrey Show, which I used as a source of moral support and courage for my future plans despite several unanswered e-mails and letters that I sent her. Only God knew if those e-mail addresses were right, but I never wavered. If you would ask me, I would say a lot of things happened that were unimaginable and unexpected, but there were a lot of ugly retaliations as well.

At this point the fear of being sent home was still very eminent. I didn't want to be looked at as a failure who travelled to the States and did not make it. Suddenly it dawned on me, what do I have to lose? Tell your tale to someone, so I did and was referred to an attorney whom I gave a call. I then made an appointment and at my arrival discovered he was a guy I met in the elevator once with my husband. He was from my tribe, and my husband had told me stories about him later. "Who cares what transpired between them? All I needed now is a savior to rescue me," I said to myself. I poured my heart to him. Surprisingly the young lawyer appeared to believe my stories. He promised to help me with my immigration issue. For his privacy, I would refer him as Attorney O. It was to be for free. He also told me about the consequences of the INS refusal to help, but I could not give a hoot. He proceeded with my case, and then I conceived my second child. Then, I was scheduled for an interview somewhere in Washington DC for my asylum claim, which was not granted. I was then referred to Baltimore. Then at this point my husband got involved and told me to drop my tribal lawyer that was helping me. If I went on with attorney O., our marriage would be over, just like when I was also threatened when I had my first son. He said if I put the name long agreed before my son's birth on the birth certificate, then the marriage would be over. The threats were nonstop, but for the fear of the unknown, I had to obey. I truly and faithfully wanted the marriage to work, although in all indication there was no marriage. So what? It would not hurt to try for the marriage to work. He was going to introduce me to his lawyer, who was very good, he said. He was a Nigerian as well by the name of Attorney E.A. I obeyed because I wanted to stay married and not to be a disappointment to my parents and family. I dropped the lawyer and relied on my husband and his lawyer to see me through. What a mistake. Even my clansman had to assist me financially to pay for this lawyer. I remembered vividly his telling me that it would be good if my husband would help because with his license he could not even represent me or practice in Baltimore, but if I needed financial assistance I could come to him. What a good man, I thought, with no strings attached. He was sympathetic with me, but I realized I could not ask him for any more help because my husband would not be pleased if he would find out that his so-called enemy is the one assisting me.

I had my second son just a few days before my first appearance in Baltimore, and his so-called lawyer had advised him to go with me to the immigration court and ask the judge for another hearing date, but we never made it there on time and was deported in absinthial. That was the beginning of my second phase of dilemma that has now lasted for decades. We then visited the lawyer from then on who made efforts and promises for a miracle, but nothing good turned out. My greatest shock was when this attorney was supposed to show up in court, but he was late. The judge, bitter and disappointed in him, addressed him in the court for messing up my case. After several opportunities that were given, he asked him to choose either for me to be interviewed on political asylum or to voluntarily depart, and Attorney E. A. opted for voluntary departure. I was dumbfounded and asked him why he did that while he was certain I could not possibly go back to Nigeria with two little boys. His words were "I will fix it before the deadline." I waited for a positive outcome but to no avail. I decided to seek help elsewhere by discussing with my co-workers at Sunrise. One Ms. Dee suggested I visit her very good lawyer at Wheaton by the name of Johnson. Yes, he would have been a good lawyer if I had the money to spend randomly without any fixed charge. The amount came as you go on a daily, hourly, and monthly basis. I was later told after a week that the credit card check that I had given the attorney for two thousand was used up and more money was required of me. Why was I not told about this from the beginning, that it was pay as you go? How and why was I in this predicament, and how could I afford such a lawyer? I was no criminal but was on a mere quest for a better world and lifestyle. I must have desired a better life but never bargained for this. It was none of what I envisioned. The American dream turned into a heartache caused by a man who professed love. What a misuse of the four-letter word. It was outside of God's way. I sometimes wondered if the American stress brought the beast out of the man that had gone and done heaven knows what to bring me to my dream country, United States of America. There are so many unanswered questions.

"What can I do?" At this moment I was a single mother with a pay of few dollars an hour. I was given favorable attention in almost all areas but money, and as a result Johnson could not represent me any longer. I fought my battles alone, as I moved out of my estrange husband's life in August of 1998. From then onward, there was no fighting, slapping around, and name calling. The situation was peaceful, but it was more difficult financially and sometimes unbearable.

The journey became cumbersome as I am left to raise two boys alone. Yes, there were a lot of ill feelings for things done against each other, but not in a million years will I abandon my sons. Their father did, however, as he fled the country to our motherland Nigeria to avoid child support.

Sometimes I wondered, would life have been better for the boys if I had endured the abuse? God forbid, I believe I would have been a statistics of those women being killed or maimed by their abusers, and mine would have probably gone undetected by the law based on my legal status. The sad aspect of it is that no one seemed to care because I was an alien. In difficult times I applied for food stamps. I was approved sixteen dollars per child each month, and for me it was not enough. What an awful experience as an immigrant. "Why should I accept such amount of money from the government?" I said to myself. "What would I buy with that?" While pondering on that, I received another letter stating that the food stamp has been increased to twenty-four dollars per child. What a life. I cried on some days nonstop, and I vowed never to receive such help from the department of social services. I would rather ask for help on the street than to receive such a meager income as help from the state for my children. First their father left the country to his motherland to avoid child support. Now the government offered me such little help. I would rather just continue to cry unto my God, who is the author and finisher of my faith. Although I have erred several times, He is still my God and in Him I would always trust. My God saw us through as He favored me in the eyes of my employer. In the late nineties, I applied at Maxim Healthcare Services as a certified nursing assistant and was hired and remained employed by Maxim for years. Wherever they sent me for a job, I was retained. That was how I managed with my two sons.

As though that was not enough, when George W. Bush came to power in the twentieth century, I contacted a lawyer to see if my immigration case should be ratified. Reviewing my case, he said yes, but I needed to hire a pro bono lawyer since I do not have the finances. He gave me few numbers. I called, and one of the few by the name of John G. returned my call and gave me an appointment to meet with him, which I did. He was wonderful and trustworthy and told me upfront that my case would not be a pro bono, but it would cost me twenty-four hundred, and I accepted. Then he went further to ask how I was going to pay it, and I responded I would try by God's grace, and I truly did. The good news was that he made the necessary efforts and gave some guidelines on how to go about it. I then approached my employer for sponsorship, and without any second thought, he said, "Ngozi, anything for you." He asked, "What does it take?" God bless you, Tony B. That's all I could say. That was the beginning of another roller coaster. This venture lasted for almost ten years. Step one was to go through the labor department, and after few years my labor certification was approved. Then came the next step for freedom and the long-anticipated liberation by the immigration, but liberation and freedom only come from God. As the Bible states in the book of John 8:36, "if the Son shall set you free, you would be free indeed." Freedom, I believe, truly comes from our redeemer. So we should be careful about how we live our lives, for the alms of men would fail, and for man's promises are vain. Only God's words and promises stand, either rain or sun.

Then came the next political phase of my immigration status that took several twists and turns. There were several demands from immigration to my employers, and they met almost all that was requested of them. Even after Tony left the company, his predecessors were true to their promise to help me reside legally in the greatest country of the world. Jason, John, and Mike—they all tried—and finally the good news came around about 2009 when I was approved by immigration for change of status. The joy of finally visiting home after almost twenty years of being an alien in a foreign land was overwhelming. The pain of having lost my dad two years earlier without being able to go home resulted with challenging questions that waited ahead when I could finally visit Oshiugbokor together with my sons comforting. Interestingly enough, my joy a few months later turned into sorrow as four immigration officers knocked on my door during the early morning of February 5, 2009. The shock was that they claimed they have been looking for me. "Why?" I asked, because I had been contacting immigration, asking for help even when things were hard. "How could they claim that they have been looking for me?" I asked. Finally, I was ordered to come to Baltimore that morning at 9:00 a.m., which I did. Life has never been the same since then, and the amazement of it all was that they told me when I got to their office that they made a mistake on my labor certification approval. What a price! Why me? I cried. The thought of giving up sometimes crept in, but my sons and God Almighty were my rock on a daily basis, knowing that I was abused by my so-called husband and the system as well. What a life of an immigrant, which I would not wish to anyone. My quest for a better future and city life turned out to be a nightmare as I struggled for survival on a daily basis with my children, and the thought of the family I left behind ate me up slowly. I knew that I would never give up my motherly care for anything in the world. This and others as the world saw the pain of leaving your motherland to the unknown world for the chase and dreams of a better life. This and all have taught me to always walk with God and never lose faith, meditate in the word, make sure my plan was in line with the word before I ventured in any and every aspect of my life. My disobedience to the word of God came with grievous consequences and a lot of hardships. Now I know that not all that glitters is gold, and our past cannot be reversed, but we need to face the future to teach and educate others of our life experiences. This is to prevent other people from making the same mistakes we had made in our past, although mistakes can never be avoided as long as man is in the flesh and the heart of man is concerned. However, we can avoid the obvious ones as we look before we leap.

Braces of the Time

Ho and ha-ha was how it all started
Walking and racing to the braces
Jumping into the paradise of braces
Wondering about the wondrous braces
Tarried as though worth the jump

Oh, how ho-ho and ha ha
Now the ha-ha becomes the hey, hey
What a deceit lies within the braces
Though they appear real,
But the real is remarkable

The change and chase of time
Oh, what a brace that lies within
Buried within the heart's chambers
Lies the unfelt but desired
Warmth is the brace so much desired.

Daddy Dearest

To my dad who passed on to eternity. This poem was written in 2007.

Daddy will live forever
Gentle kind tender and loving
True to his belief, sometimes heavy-handed
Slowly showed life's path
Fast like a cheetah, tireless as a tiger
Slippery and smooth as a dolphin
Daddy dearrest, how time flies
Parting from Dad is bitter
Absent in presence, together in spirit
Why? why? Nature, why?
Daddy, it's not meant to be, no, not this way
How life has twisted fate
Always firm in faith unto eternity
Sail on, fly like the eagles
Fly on, Daddy dearest, fly unto glory
We shall one day, some day, anchor
Unto that glorious plane
Victory is sure, Daddy dearrest
Goodbye, Papa, till we meet again.

Dream

To every dreamer out there:

How relentless and frequent,
Real are your mysteries and loosely most often
What lies within thee after all
Vision of the unquenchable mind
Dragging the untold stories

Sometimes draining, confusing, peacefull, welcoming
Dwells within the state of being
Complicated, complex lies, hidden messages
Who is who to interpret how far you've come?
Conditions untold, driven by state of mind

Driving, draining, dry not the weak mind
How common, mindfull matching as you stroll
Mysteries lie beneath your route
Highly rated what an entity
Visit less often and frequent no more

Determination

Arise, oh, my soul
Wake up from thine deep slumber
Slumber not for time is come
Joy for moment and love why you can
Why sleep on a lonely road
Prepare thy path and may the true love reign
The hours and times unknown
But the true love conquers it all
Wake up and fight for your right
Protect that that needs protection
Preserve those that need preservation
Slumber no more as the good Lord backs you up.

Fear

Once you were far away,
Never mentioned amongst queens
Why suddenly appear
Flee, flee from this kingdom
Engulf and trample her not

Descend not, why so sudden
Who gave thee permission
Bought and bright is her sweet mind
Why visit without invitation
Relinquish your grips

Release, rejoice not over her
Depart, oh, depart Mr. Fear
Dissappear into the deep dark sea
Bought and brave is her soul and spirit
Flee, oh, fear, and visit no more.

Freedom

In freedom we pray,
In freedom we preach,
In freedom we pool,
In freedom we plant,
In freedom we pleasure,
Therefore, freedom pending, peace
unreached.
In freedom we plan,
In freedom we publish,
In freedom we ponder,
In freedom we pursue,
In freedom we preserve,
Therefore, in peace we attain freedom.
In freedom we perish,
In freedom we pay,
In freedom we partake,
In freedom we progress,
In freedom we participate,
Therefore, oh freedom beget peace.

Father

Father, oh Father!
You provided fuel for the car,
You drove home safely
You made it get to its destination,
You cleaned and maintained it,
You dared anyone's encroachment,
Safely it was driven.
Oh, Father, you truly are our father.
I could not ask differently.

Friendship

(Dedicated to Brother Seto for Sister Darcas N.)

What a bond of brotherly love,
Rooted as it was heavenly made,
Incredible moments shared,
Excellency in God was the start.

Newness of heart built joyous moments,
Dedicated to the holy calling,
Surviving the wallows of time,
Holding to the true testimonies,

In excellency we found another,
Anchoring to the true nature of God,
Greatly gracing the being of us
Farewell, my beloved friend,

Soon someday soon we shall
We truly shall meet again
Sail on, my beloveth friend, sail on!
Glory in Abraham's bosom as you sleep,

Eminent endowing is our friendship,
Hold on to it as you sleep,
I would, should certainly hold on,
Till we meet again I say good-bye!

Faith

How twisted, sometimes hopeless
Yes, exists filled with doubts
Aspired, far-fetched
Desired, easily forgotten

Longed for, deeply dreaded
Cherished, sometimes mourned
Judged, soon abandoned
Reached, most times dropped

Faith, where art thou
Why have thou gone thus far?
Bring forth thy aroma
Cheer up the dead

Restore the broken spirit
Restore the weak bone
Restore the sleepy mind
Awaken the dead spirit

Oh, faith how desired
Stand firm to thy testimonies
Oh, faith how real
Pure and tested art thou.

God's Grace 1

The grace of God flows like an ocean,
It flows to and fro the earth,
So much so deep and wide,
Enduring the sinful nature of man,
Mightier than the love of a mother,
Unconditionally pushing and pulling,
Though our sins seemed unpardonable,
His grace swallows them all,
Thank goodness for the grace of God.

God's Grace 2

Sandy, searchable, avails for all
Greener than the green grass
Grows within and around
Beautifully surrounded in mercy
What a marvelous gift
Branded infinitesimal
Distributed as it is reachable
Oh, what an awesome gift
Enriching as it endows
Oh, what a wondrous grace!
The grace of God
Reaching out for everyone
Receive, retain, and review
What an ocean of grace
That is available for all.

Global Dance

We all imagine dancing in unison
What language steps to emulate
Versed filled with cultural norms and values
Cultivated are the norms and values
Whose norms values dot dialects

To be used as the globe is multicultural
How do we implement our rhythm?
Steps and stands as we dare and dream
Universal dance attainable if practiced
Proving and adopting to be the right moves

Who knows if we could and would?
No harm in trying, the rest had to surrender
Theirs and learn to focus and adopt one
Which could be the best global dance
For the ultimate global dance

Gold

Mom and Dad Chief and Mrs. Selinah Gad Umajie and my
sons, Joe and Jr.

Oh, how precious you are!
Preserved and never loses her value
Beautiful gold
How precious you are

Desired by many
Used up by her beauty
Buried in the depth of the sea
Down in the ocean bed

Waiting for a rescue
Wait a little bit longer
Oh, gold wait, while we search
Help is on the way.

Heaven

Oh, heaven how mysterious!
Observed, pointed, and watched by all
Desiring it is few feet away
Oh, heaven how mysterious!
Covers as it shadows all
Looks as it appears few feet away
Oh, heaven how mysterious!
Internalised and sort by all,
Oh, heaven, where are thou?
Surrounded by mysteries of life
Oh, heaven, where are thou
How magnificent
Moves farther as we approach
Oh, heaven, thy mysteriesly within
thee.

H*** In Paradise

Smiley, smooth, swift, she walked,
Bags and baggages stuffed.
Got into the aircraft,
What a crafty experience!
Wondered what lies ahead.
Bumpy was the ride filled with joy.
Lost all her youthful vigor.
Visualizing the unseen,
How misinformed and misjudged,
Sorrow unpredicted.
What an adventurous moment.
Jumped journeyed and joggled,
Hoping sometime soon,
The true tales of paradise would
surface.

His Mercies

His mercies are forever
We run away from him
His mercies bring us back
We sin continuosly
His mercies abound
We sometimes stray
His mercies unfold
We stray uncontrollably
Yet His mercies are unstoppable
We wonder numerous ways
His mercies retrieve
We swim sometimes in sin
His mercies swam farther
We dance with the devil often
Yet His mercies abound
Oh, how merciful is our God.

What A Life

Friends and foes, cheers and woes
Days and nights come and go
Yet our minds stay frozen
Do we appreciate the little things
And ignore the big things or do?
We roam in life, without a clue
Do we embrace the things that make us frown?
And push away the laughter
Or do we always think situations through
And never think what could happen after?
Simplicity always comes in a complex form
And the strongest wrongs are always norm
So despite the understanding we think we had
And the emotions we go through—happy, angry, or sad
There is always this question that will cause us strife . . .
What is *Life*?

—Joseph F. Ukwu

Wonders of the Jungle

Quiet, cute, and cozy
Cold, breezy, most muddy,
Living the jungle life
Living as though in paradise

All natural habitats,
Nakedness, a natural norm,
Siting of wilds natural,
Exciting wild windy breeze

Songs of birds soothin'
Nature regulates man's existence,
Beautiful jungle, retain
Oh, retain thine naturality!

Joy

Oh, joy where have you gone?
Where is thine aroma?
How far have you gone?
Wondering the beauty of thine taste
Perfect in thine existence,
Desires to wallow in thine presence,
Preserving the memories of the past.
Oh, joy return to thy temple,
Thou unbreakable link, return, oh, return,
The thread that holds the center,
Oh, joy what a treasure!
The reason for existence returns,
Disappear no more and lead as usual,
Occupy, dine, and tarry in your abode
So the soul may be joyful again.

Life

What is she after all, watching as it
began
Sometimes unnoticed, sometimes
unexpected
Yet there she is, sometimes blooms
Sometimes unexplainable, how
mysterious?

Strong, sometimes weary, how
misunderstood
What a four-lettered entity, mightier
than all
Filled with hopes and dreams
Fullfilled by least most insignificance

Sometimes foiled by the woes of her
youth
How magnificent is her existence
Life, what a beauty, what a mystery
Live on, the untold lies within thee.

Loneliness

Oh! what a shuttle!
How suddenly saddled.
Shamed, shredded, also dreaded,
Mingled in the misty shades.

Loneliness, walk away.
Disappear while the day approaches,
Run while the night near,
Cold ceases the coverless body

What a bullet!
Deadlier than imagined
Sometimes possesses the serpent venom
Lingers even more at the darkest hour.

Oh, loneliness advance no more.
Depart, depart, and never return
Retreat with your poisonous grips
Advance and return no more.

Love

Oh, how sweet is thy name
How used is thy name
Wondering who you are
Sometimes misinterpreted
How misused is thy name
What are you after all?
Beautiful love how cheerful
Walking in the mix of cloud
Oh love, who are thou really?
Tell the world and show thyself
Speak out and be thou exposed
How misused are thou
Love will always be victorious
The reason for existence
Love, how beautiful art thou
Always victorious and conquerous

Life's Uncertainty

Sometimes the weather appears gloomy
Sometimes very bright
Other times unpredictable
The reality is that the sun sets
She also rises at her own pace

The weatherman predicts
But the end result is uncertain
The rain may fall as it's predicted
He jubilates for the end result
While in reality it was just an event to happen

It may fall cat and dog
This in essence boosts his ego
At his prediction we all may get anxious
And excited but tomorrow they say is pregnant
So why the boost anyway?

Why predictions, dreams, and camouflages,
The complexities of life are sometimes beyond comprehension
If there be a fact, it is that life is unpredictable
And the mysteries of life are far-fetched as we travel within
With or without the body as we sleep

Some may wonder the complexities
But why wonder uncertainties?
Why try to control that which is uncontrollable?
Sometimes as humans we may try and succeed
The complex entity of life is our weak and greatest

The appearance of the day may be bright
Colorful, wholesome, and sometimes peaceful
His predictions may be wonderfully accurate
But the weatherman can only assume
The certainty of it all lies with the mysteries of life.

Lioness and her Cubs

Lioness, what a beautiful creature,
Bonded, beauty boldly visible
Hunts vigorously for her cubs
Tentatively bravely chases for meals
Admired for her courage and strength.

Looks far beyond her vicinity
Dedicates and searches for prey,
Smells and snoozes for food as hunger is inevitable
Roars minimally as per the male,
Hunting faithfully for her cubs

Protecting her cubs without reservations,
No limit to her strength towards her cubs
What a gift of nature as the cubs glow
No limit to her guide and warmth
Beautiful cubs of a brave lioness,

Her beauty seen and shared with her cubs,
Provision and protection grow viciously
Lining and living with the care of the lioness
Hunts singly with lack of peers backup
Live forever, oh, lioness, as courage admired!

Mountain of Thought

Searched for direction,
She climbed the top,
Successfully reached the peak,
Wondered how uncomfortable,
Chose to hang on,
Thought of climbing down,
No, decided to stay
Wished the thought would flow
Swamped, swimming are the thoughts,
Yes, now more than ever,
Oh, mountain, how misjudged you are.
Thoughts now overwhelming,
Hardly could stare down,
There appears Mr. Phobia,
Why climb the mountain after all?
Wishing she was at the base,
No! No! No regrets in trying,
Adventure accomplished as thought
overflows.

Mirror in the Homes

The distance that seperates loved once due to uncontrollable circumstance

What an invention!
Sometimes deceitful and decent,
Pictures even not needed.
Needed even at a distance.

Becomes part of every household,
Beautifully attached to every home,
Appreciated but missleading sometimes.
Detasted, sometimes wondering how.

So often wondering, what an invention?
Images appear not to be held
Oh, mirror, how useful, desirable, and monopolized
Images sometimes appear as much as they dissappear

Wishing you were real
Shaped shiny and smooth
Glistering like a glowing star
Mirror, oh, mirror, what an invention.

Mother

Mother, oh, mother!
The miracle of mankind
The origin of companion
The taste of mercy
The holder of the home

Mother, oh, Mother!
The energizer of us all
The order of the universe
Trainer of us all
Helper of the fetus

Mother, oh, mother!
The egg bearer of mankind
The salt of life
Love undoubted
Teacher of us all

Mother, receive rejoice
The universe is in contempt
As Mother carries, cuddles
The unborn till and forever
Mother, oh mother, what a diamond!

My Lost Love

Dedicated to Mr Kingsley Nwouche:
Sleeping and swimming, wondering
How soft and succulent is the touch
Thrilled running down the rainy vibes
Short and swift lies the period
Whereby an hour seemed like seconds
Thought it was a meaningful magic
So it seemed seasonally,
Walking into an empty bed still
Seemed warm and wanted,
How time flew in the misty wind
Wondering and wishing we could
bring back time and start all over
As one wishes, yesterday will
return our lost love.

Mr. and Mrs. Pure

All believers that desire to live wholly for Christ:

> Pushing and pulling to the point of purity
> Quite a distance
> Travelled far and wide for purity
> Accross the sea ocean land and space
>
> What a distance
> Often thougt attainable but slightly dropped
> Though thought and desired
> The goal of purity unreachable and unrealistic
>
> One should not give up but keep pressing
> By his grace and mercies purity attainable
> As we honestly push and press forward
> Purity attainable by His grace.

Orbit of Life

Life is unique as you can observe.
Swimming like a fish starts the journey.
Sometimes sluggish and most times swift.
Daring to make his first move,
Sometimes clumsy and weary.
Numerous steps but one at a time.
Some dare to circle it all,
Some wish to stop in the middle,
Many try several times.
Some succeed at an attempt.
Others with trillion.
Dare not to surrender.
Start your round-trip with a step.
Some walk, others race
In all, everyone will circle the orbit.

Progression

Though I tear profusely
The tears are profounded.
Though I walk gorgeously
The walks are guided.

Though I smile seasonlessly
The smiles are seasoned.
Though I speak randomly
The speeches are right.

Though I provide endlessly
The provisions are endowed.
Though I sing softly
The songs are empowered.

Though the sores ooze
The healing is perfected.
Praise to Him that heals
Preciously available to all.

Peace

She is given as it is attainable
Spreads as it germinates
Waters as it soothes
Starts from the Master giver
Received by the lowly
Spreads wings like the eagle
Flies far and wide as it determines
Generates the ultimate
Begins from the very root
That brightens each day
Oh, peace, be thou fulfilled
The joy of the home as it spreads
Oh peace, spread that mankind!
Live as she enjoys her planet earth.

Pain

Dedication to this poem is a result of my difficult times in this life's
journey.
She is constantly seldomly visible
Soothes as though a necessity
Shields as though needed
Shelter no more departure eminent

Strenghens in her weakness
Stretches even beyond border
Strokes as never before
Stood as it endeavors

Seldomly selfishly departs
Slowly realeases the restless
Strikenly unbearable and undesirable
Stop, oh, pain, crawl no more.

Prices for All

Yes, there are prices for everyone.
Sometimes immediate and at times prolonged
Yet everyone desires and deserves it.
Yes, we all advocate and advance toward it
Sometimes prudent and attainable

Sometimes recommended
Some pinch push and punch
Yet it awaits us all
Some speak loud quick for theirs
Push and pin for the ultimate

Oh, what a price!
Drum and dream for the unquenchable
Yes, the migthier than thou
Seek and sort the splendid
What a price that awaits us all.

Tranquility that exists in the face of adversities when you trust God.

Restores peace and quietness
Rests on a peaceful sleep
Sleeps as though she lives no more
Snores as though no one hears

Admires the sounds of the rain
Adores the sounds of her drops
As images appear insgnificant
Aspires to impact the visions of the weary

Never stop, oh, rain
Never cease your drops
Peaceful soul sows as she drops
Rain, how peaceful art thou.

Rainbow

Symbolic is thy angelic appearance
Radiant is thy rounded robust image
Incredible is the tale of thy existence
As the symbol of God's love eminent

Obvious reminder of God's love for mankind
Neatly noted is thy call
Bowing to thine maker beautiful rainbow
Oh, what a testimony of God's love!

Well done, sail on beautiful rainbow
Gone for a short while
We would behold thee again
Sweet, holy rainbow what a covenant

Fulfilled in the mercy of God
As you radiantly stood above all
What a great and wonderful reminder
God's love is made perfect in you.

Hello, thou art great symbol
Leave on and light thine candle
High above the planet earth
As we glow in thy testimonies.

Swimming in an Ocean

I swim in an ocean.
I swim anyway
knowing that he that swims with
me is the creator of the ocean.
I swim with swift slippery ocean species.
I swim anyway knowing the creator swims along anyway.
Though I wonder what lies within the ocean.
I wonder less anyway
knowing the controller swims with me at all times anyway.

Sweet Rose

Spiky, smoothe rose,
Wondering the worth of thee,
Energizing aroma of thine presence,
Endowing the joy of so many
Treated with kindness as a symbol of love
Rooted but lasted for a few
Observing the preservation of love
Soaked as emerged in the ocean of love
Your empathy touches all hearts.

Sweet Patience

Oh, sweet Patience,
At the mention of your name,
Peace and tolerance found.
Touching and teaching intelligently.
Excellent in newness of time,
Caring and enduring all things,
Sometimes overwhelming.
Oh, patience, what an endowment.
Longing for the peace that emerges within.
Admits the weakness of man,
Talks independently with wisdom,
Excellent, noble, and calm
Endures the newness of heart,
Oh, patience, what a golden name.

Simple life

Oh, what a simple life,
Shows up with humility
Embraces all things
Walks as though there's no worry

Sometimes devoted to her course
Dances at all tunes of music
Appreciates nature's endowments
Learns lives and leans within

Steps into satisfaction smoothly
Sees as though not seen
Joggles sometimes less intense
Sometimes outcome misread

Tell me and the rest about it all
Some may monitor and mock
Simple may seem well taken
Always desire and cling to it.

What a window of wisdom
Cherished and cheered by many
Oh, what a simple life
Yes, live and drink every ounce of it.

Tears of Threat

The face glows as the tears flow
Dropping like a ball of hail
Slowly running down the cheeks
Checking which and what direction
Slowly drools down the rug
Soaked with the hailish drops
Is the rugged rug
Mopping and pondering what a treat
As the tears keep pouring
Wondering what a threat
As the flow continued without consolations
Unanswered questions prompt, doubt to the laws of nature
As tears flow salted it seemed.

The Flesh of Man

Serves as a glow for the individuals,
Protects as it seems, and luring.
Sometimes seen as physical,
It entails more than the luring attributes.
Stands on her own, demanding,
Sometimes pushes to the top of her demands
Appears to control the man's nature,
Longs for the rebellious attributes of hers,
Dreaded as it fights with the spirit nature,
Warring sometimes so it seems,
Dragging the unfulfilled thoughts and desires,
Thou launches at forbidden territories.
Most times seems unstoppable,
Oh, flesh, what are you made up of?
Thy wirings are controlled only by thine ultimate,
So, flesh, stop rebelling and bow.
Thou art subject to the ultimate authority.

The Scorn of the Snake

Snuggled slowly, rounds its prey
Scolged bulgy eyes
Lies the unexpected prey
Struggled for air seemed far-fetched
Strokes stroden with little left
Sputum appeared unstoppable
Slowly visualizing the unpredictable
Wondered for a wondrous rescue
Tapping, treading the unbearable pain
Though it seemed at a time
Stupidly indulged in a rescue attempt
Farther, further been scorned
Suddenly emerges the ultimate rescue
Beholding the powerlessness of a man
Shouted with a loud voice
Thou ultimate rescuer behold
Thine servant sinketh
Uphold thine sinking servant
Suddenly soothingly releases her grips
There comes her second chance.

The Pivotal Walk

Walking on a beautiful road,
Sometimes paces to finish,
On such a meandering road,
Vital vial is the walk,
Energy consumed worthwhile,
Journey of three seemed six,
Pulping, inhaling the misty wind,
Subsequently running into walkers,
Some enjoyed their walk it seemed,
What an architectural beauty,
Wondering when and how but continued,
Seldomly proceeds as the legs tingle,
Walk enjoyed as relaxation eminent,
At last there comes its reward.

The Golden Gate

Such a mythical beautiful gate,
Searching tirelessly and endlessly,
So much desired and dreamt about
Searching so much that to some is a reality
Such that to others is just a myth,
Oh, what a nature that viewing is dimensional
Why can't we all view and ascertain?
The reality of the golden gate
Such a desirable golden gate,
Shining as it may seem tantalizing,
So we keep pursuing the desired mythical gate,
Keep pursuing as the mythical may eventually
Turn to reality as the search continues,
Endlessly runs like the blue sea,
Beautifully made, the content unexplainable,
Oh, what an awesome gate to walk through.

The Love Of God

His love is incomparable
His love is beyond measure
Flows beyond and above man's imagination
Travels faster than the thunder and lightning
Flows like the blue ocean
Deeper than the depth of the sea
Quickens and touches the weakest of all
Exalts the meekest of us all
Blows our fire as it enlightens
Heats as it moves the unmovable

Travels millions of miles to share
Flows and reaches the undesirable
Walks in the darkest links
The companion undesirable
Watches as it engulfs man's weakness
Wonders for the rescue of the lost
Restores the unrecoverable
Oh, what an Excellency!
Welcomes the lonely and deserted
Pursues beyond man's comfortability
Touches the untouchable
Oh, what a love!
Come embrace the pure and ever lasting
What a great and marvelous love
Gracious granted and great is His love.

Thief on Plain Cloth

A thief moves around
Plainly strolling the street
Surely with confidence
Targeting her prey
Politely luring the unexpected
Tone undaunted with glamorous smile
Speech spontaneous, flawless
Still minding her victims
The unknown and defenseless
Walking on a lonely path
Pondering on the cashless
Fearing the recognized shadow
In a plain cloth thought worthless
Just for a moment realizes
The relentless power of the
Plain cloth thief
Sure, he who targets the weakling
Would one day have his day,
In the supreme court that only
Stands for the truth
So help the defenseless, Mighty One.

The Church Of Holiness

Walked into the church
Women, men, and children visibly holy.
Winked at him, realizes holiness
abound,
Sprung on my feet with holy
excitement.
Walking, clapping, singing, and
dancing.
Jumping most times depicts holiness.
Wishing the holiness unstoppable.
Prayed as though departing unto glory.
Eternity eminent as portrayed.
Listerning to the word and thought
Fantastic,
What a perfect message.
Longing for the long-lasting holliness.
Lasted but within the church's vicinity.
Help us, oh, Master Supreme.
That our holy cravings will succeed.
Though realistically we often slide,
The church of holiness will succeed.

The Word

Shoots, sharp and shines,
Wisdom forever with the word.
Shows the path to life internal,
Soothes as though physical.
Smooths the path for peace,
Survives the trend of time.
Sows even in a dry land,
Saves the brokenhearted.
Sustains the wanton soul
Shift as it grows amongst thorns
Swift, sweet, and sits within
Mighty and powerful is the word.

The Golden Shore

All those who are struggling on daily basis to make it.

There is a golden shore
There it glows as it glitters
Attractive is the shore
Admired as it seemed

Walking on the golden shore
Wears out the instep
Although very vast it appears
Wondering what's the drive

Sore sole blisters uncontrollably
Soaked as it appears pale
Searching for a soothed shore
Swimming within the beautiful shore

Shining as the star
Oh, what a shore!
Reflects the beauty of the sea
Though painful but soothing.

The Walk of Man

To all believers:

In the very tiny beginning was man.
Swimming as embedded in the womb.
Emerged into an immaculate world,
Man had never ceased the walk outside his creator.
Sometimes he walks upright,
Ninety-nine percent of the time opposite,
Though rescued by the sacrificial lamb.
Man will always be man.
Most times struggles to walk straight.
Truly there's no man in this holy walk.
Man remains man even unto eternity.
Real man's true desire is to walk right with God.
Although, man's true nature is sin.
Oh, Sacrificial Lamb, help man with his struggles!
Oh, Majesty, help man with his working sinful walk!

The Death of a Righteous Man

(Dedicated to Dr. T. V. Erekosima)

THOUGH IT IS PAINFUL,
IT PLEASES THE HEART.
THOUGH SOMETIMES CONFUSING,
IT CONSOLES THE SAINTS.
THOUGH SOMETIMES COMFORTING,
IT CONFUSES THE WEARY.
THOUGH IT BLISTERS THE SOULS,
TREMENDEOUSLY BLESSES THE SAINTS.
OH, WHAT A FULFILLED APPOINTMENT!
AS HIS FOOTPRINT LIVES ON,
WHAT A LIFE OF TESTIMONIES,
WHAT A LIFE TO REMEMBER,
REMINDING US ALL BOLDLY, BOASTFULLY, BEAUTIFULLY
WHAT A FOOTPRINT TO EMULATE, AS THE SPIRIT LIVES ON
TO GLORY!

The Heart of Man

Who would be wise enough?
Who would be watchful enough?
Who would be willing enough?
Who with wisdom enough
Dilate the heart of man,
The underlining muscles of the heart,
That beautifully designed.
Who can determines the heart of man?
Whose interpretations are far-fetched?
Predictions unknown
Oh, what lies within thee
That even the wisest dare not.
Oh, who would dare interpret
The heart of man?
What beautiful, deceitful creation.

The Young Heart

The heart of the young beauty desires perfection
The perfect heart is far-fetched.
The journey yet unknown
As beauty's heart is deeply wounded.

Oh, beauty, why have you wondered?
The desires of thy heart are like an endless journey.
Oh, beauty, why has thou gone astray?
Turn and see that the heart longs for a perfected beauty.

Why long for the heart that desires no beauty?
Create thy path for the unknown journey.
Let the heart be embedded with her desires.
Then the goal for a perfect heart arrives.

The Path

Freely trodden is the path
Healing wholesomeness awaits
Immaculate without schism
Pure, prudent invitations

Tranquility tenderly tracheid
Holy awesomeness is the path
Amazing merciful movement
Oh, beauty, what a freedom!

Good-bye to schism, wholesomeness reigns
Oh, what an endowing path!
Awesome, wholesome healing
The unshakable prudent invitation

Movement ever so smooth
Welcoming is the path
Tenderly, triumphantly overflows
Awesome God, what a gift
Freedom of movement
Smoothness incomparable
Warmth unquenchable
Glows twenty-four-seven

Obstructions none
Out busting in its Holiness
Glowing is the golden path
What an awesome path.

The Irreversible Clock

Silent Voice

She was a very vibrant young damsel who was born in a very remote countryside called Oshiugbokor Village. The place of her birth is described as remote compared to that of the modern cities around her vicinity. She grew up in a very vibrant, energetic, God-fearing, and loving family of ten. She grew up loved, protected, provided, and cared for as the youngest baby girl of the family. In her years of growing up, she never thought or foresaw a future with loneliness, being far away from such a loving family and environment, although her thought as a youngster has always been to travel with her now-late beloved brothers to a foreign country. Her earliest dream of travelling was shattered as a result of the untimely death of Joseph because of a car accident on December 1979. It changed the joy of Christmas forever in her life.

She never gave up hope of travelling abroad. She still hoped and believed that someday her brother's dream for her would come to pass. She grew up in a village where the source of light at night is either the moonlight or lamps and lanterns, and the means of transportation is either one's feet or bicycles of one's choice. She always had in mind travelling to the cities that, she was told, had electricity, cars, and motorcycles. In her eldest's term, "the city where there is light in the sky at night and loud music played at all times, where one could hardly tell the difference between day and night." At about age eight, her first journey began. She walked miles with her feet to enable her to travel to a bigger city called Abua with her kinswomen.

It was a marriage ceremony whereby the matured single women of a family escorted their kinswoman to her new groom's home. The bride was being escorted to another village called Ochiegba, but because the journey would take them through the city, she wanted to be included. What a moment it was for her as her papa approved of it despite the fact that her mama and the rest of the women did not. It was a dream come true. That was a trip she would never forget. However, she regretted it as halfway through the journey, she asked the elders if she could go back home, but it's too late, they said. The distance was so much that a journey that was supposed to be for a day lasted for two because they were unable to walk back home the same day. She remembered crying when they said it was time to leave. Few others had sore feet the next morning, and some of them had to be assisted by their elders by carrying them on their backs. You think she would have learnt her lessons. No. Then at age ten she undertook another trip to a farther city called Ahoada, which was the only city in her Ekpeye clan. Then at age twelve, she finally resided in Ahoada with her eldest sister. Grace was very industrious as the first daughter of the family but was given out for marriage at a very young age to help her two younger brothers go to secondary school. Several times she attempted to run back home, but she would always be taken back by her parents. Then finally she settled. She lived with her for two years; lost two years of her secondary school to baby-sit for her sister's first two children, Silverline and Magnus, briefly, Mom said to me, you have to go back to school now, because to continue living with Grace would spoil me as she would not let me do no house chores but commercial engagements

The life in the city was wonderfully exciting to her. She then proceeded to high school. As standard six parents and teachers, education for their children was a priority except for the fact that the first daughter was used as a sacrificial lamb for the family's financial problem after the war. She was the only child that could not attend high school to enable her brothers to go. Their papa could not afford three school fees at the same time.

Therefore, her secondary education would not just take her away from home but to a distant city. First it was to St. Judas Girls Amarata. Then the second year earned her a transfer to Elelewa Girls. Unfortunately the school principal told her brother Nelson that they were late, that the school was already filled up, and that there would be no room for any new students. She was then left with three choices: go back to Amarata, which was a horrible experience for her; wait until next semester to go to Elelewa, or join Mary at Bodo City Girls, which was moved from County High School Ahoada. She chose the last because *she* assumed going to the same school with *her* senior sister would serve as a safe haven. She wouldn't want the torture one would usually go through in her first year. Surely it helped. This actually was the beginning of life in the city because life in Port Harcourt was truly the city life, not similar to Ahoada. That was the beginning of the loss of innocence as enjoying the city life entailed freedom of movement and access to all that life could offer, except that the choice was yours. This was where the family's upbringing played a vital role.

The only time she visited home to see her papa and mama briefly was during holidays especially Christmas. But that changed automatically after 1979. The family bond was so great that no one stayed away from home for a long period of time. Her papa—who had been the director, protector, and warrior of the home—hardly stayed away from home for a long time even during his teaching career. He could only stay at his station Mondays through Thursdays. Every Friday night, her papa would be home. Then her papa would travel back and forth daily with his bicycle if his station would not be too far from home. Grace, who had been given out for marriage, hardly stayed away from home as she constantly visited. The bitter taste of the dream was when her quest for bigger cities and her desire for international journey took her to the United States of America in 1993.

Her international journey did not equip her with the tales and details of journeying internationally. She thought in a few months, she would be back home to her parents, brothers and sisters, aunts, uncles, nephews, and nieces. What a bitter experience as she was stranded in a foreign country, and her dreams turned sour. For the love of the city, her family lost her; and for the love of children, she lost her family. Her city love cost her everything she had loved and ever known to be meaningful, which was her family. While in the foreign country in January, 2007 she lost her Dad. In the early 2000, she lost one of her younger brothers Clement, who left Robinson, the last son of the family behind. The loss of her Daddy Chief G. W. Umajie and her uncles, especially German Umajie, who was a World War II veteran was devastating. What a tragedy and sadness she never envisioned. The decade passeed by; her eyes or those of her foreign begotten children had not seen any members of their maternal family. How she wished she could turn back the time, but her past would never be recovered, and her future would never be the same. Sorrow was inevitable, but her strength comes from knowing the Lord. If Jesus is in the vessel, who can fear the storm? Her poetry work told it all. There was no place like home, whether country or city, poor or rich. There is no place like home. She wished time can turn back the clock, or she could reverse her past.

Made in the USA
Columbia, SC
12 July 2023

20366255R00043